THE WIN WIN SOLUTION

A New Approach to Co-Parenting

THE WIN WIN Solution

A New Approach to Co-Parenting

Terrell Hurston

Hurston Enterprise LLC

Copyright © 2023 Terrell Hurston

All Rights Reserved. Printed in the USA. No part of this book may be reproduced or transmitted in any form or by any means, written, electronic, recording, photocopying, or otherwise, without prior written permission of the author, Terrell Hurston. It is illegal to copy this book, post it to a website, or distribute it by any other means without permission.

Developmental Editor: Amber Hatch
Copy Editor: Abbey McLaughlin
Cover Art by Samia Asif

Library of Congress Control Number:2023908297

ISBNs:
Paperback - 979-8-9881147-0-3
Hardcover - 979-8-9881147-1-0

First Edition
Printed in the United States of America

Books may be purchased in quantity and/or special sales by contacting the author by email at: tchurston@gmail.com with 'Book Purchase' in the subject line.

Publishing Consultant:
Revision Publishing LLC
www.revisionpub.com

Disclaimer

The information presented in this book is intended for general informational purposes only. The publisher and author make no warranties, expressed or implied, regarding the accuracy, completeness, or suitability of the information contained within these pages. The content provided is based on the author's research, personal experience, and perspective.

The reader is advised to consult a professional for specific advice related to their own situation. The publisher, author, and any associated parties shall not be held liable for any loss, injury, or damage caused or alleged to be caused directly or indirectly by the information presented in this book.

Furthermore, references and citations to external sources, products, or services do not imply endorsement or recommendation by the publisher, author, or associated parties. The reader should use their own discretion when relying on such references and seek independent verification as necessary.

The information included in this book is not a substitute for professional advice. The reader should consult a licensed attorney or professional for specific legal concerns.

To Miss Nyla Symone Hurston, you gave me purpose.

Table of Contents

Disclaimer

v

Introduction

1

Chapter 1

The Child Comes First, No Matter What

9

Chapter 2

Is Arguing Even Worth It?

19

Chapter 3

Co-Parenting 101

27

Chapter 4

Boundaries

33

Chapter 5

Letting Go of the Emotions That Tie

39

Chapter 6

Shut Up and Listen

47

Chapter 7
Think Like a Coach
53

Chapter 8
The Impact of the Breakup on You
65

Chapter 9
Modeling Appropriate Behavior
75

Chapter 10
Peace
83

Acknowledgements
89

About the Author
91

THE WIN WIN *Solution*

Introduction

That one look on my daughter's face changed my whole outlook. After I saw the look on her face, I knew I had to change and do things differently for my princess. It was my defining moment—the start of my journey. I had to find out what it meant to co-parent effectively.

I remember it like it was yesterday. My daughter's mother was picking her up from my house one day. As I placed her in the car seat, her mother and I started arguing. Usually mild-mannered and even-tempered, raising my voice was out of character for me. I always took a step back to think before I spoke.

But this time was different.

I remember everything except the subject of our discussion. As we continued to disagree, we became progressively louder. I knew my back-and-forth was out of frustration. When I was buckling Nyla into her car seat, I made eye contact with her. She was almost four years old, looking at me like her world was ending.

That look stopped me dead in my tracks, and the argument was over in an instant. I went to kiss my precious baby good-bye and she resisted, like I wasn't the father she once knew. I had only just moved out. My daughter and I were used to seeing each other every morning as I had been a morning person and usually the one waiting for her to get up to play or make breakfast. Now, I wasn't seeing her every morning, and I already felt distant. When she reacted to me like that, it crushed my soul. I walked back to my apartment in a level of pain I didn't know existed. One thing was certain: I never wanted my daughter to look or feel that way about me again. My pride and ego had no space in this new norm.

I had to figure this out. I couldn't just let things slide, but I couldn't sit and protest everything. All I cared about was my daughter. Her happiness brought me happiness. Parents splitting up is hard enough on any child, and I didn't want to make it harder. I know people who experienced these situations and had long-term effects into adulthood. Hell, *I'm* one of those people. I'll be damned if I was going to add more hardship to my daughter's life.

Co-parenting is one of the best things you can do for a child living between two separate households. We brought our children into this world, whether it was planned or not. This sounds so cliché, but they didn't ask to be here. As parents, we are responsible for raising them to be good citizens and knowing what love and support feel like from the people closest to them.

I realized as I got older how that was what I craved the most. I wanted that positive reinforcement to battle the negative self-talk as a shy and reserved kid. I imagine any child wants and craves that from their parents. I also resolved at eleven years old that I would be a better parent. At the time, I didn't even know what "better" looked like, but I knew it had to be better than what I had experienced. I also knew kids who were in way worse situations than me. Even though my childhood was rocky, I still considered myself lucky because I had my Granny, and I wasn't getting beaten or molested. But I didn't have it easy, and that gave me a hard exterior, like nothing was bothering me, but that wasn't true. I was missing my mom deeply, and the what-ifs haunted me; they still do.

Sometimes I feel that people should see things the way I see them and that since I have a good heart, they should go with what I say. Even though I have and operate from a good heart, this is delusional thinking. The world doesn't revolve around me, and I can't expect people to conform.

Introduction

I've always known I was a good and honest person whose moral compass is out of this world. Well, at least compared to my childhood environment. I always knew I wanted to make an impact, and not just in my immediate community. I wanted to reach further.

So many people in this world live in situations similar to mine, raising children in two separate households. I knew I had something to offer. Co-parenting can be the hardest thing in the world or the easiest. To me it's the perspective parents choose. I certainly can't emphasize enough that it is not one-size-fits-all. Everyone's situation is different. Effective co-parenting hasn't been demonstrated often, so I honestly think parents just don't know what it can look like. I certainly didn't.

A lot of break-ups result in hurt feelings and broken communication, but when children are involved, every decision we make affects them.

As a child, I was on the receiving end of that fallout, and now, as a father, my mission was to shield my daughter from everything I had endured. It was like I was taking all the bullets for her so she wouldn't have to feel anything I felt. Why would I subject someone I love to the same pain I had been subjected to?

Our children are the most precious possessions we are responsible for, and far too often, they are at the bottom of the totem pole while our ego and pride rests at the top. This is a common problem, and this was my problem. I'll be the first to admit I let my pride and ego call the shots. They told me when and how to react, which level my voice should be, and they told me how far to go. But it never told me how to get what I required. And from that, my child and I suffered. No matter how "right" I was, I was losing, and the more my daughter saw this, the more I was losing her. I could not let that happen.

I wrote this book because I know how it feels to be that child wanting to see my parents get along. I know how it feels to be at the bottom of the totem pole, knowing the unfavorable outcomes from their actions I'd experience. But I also know firsthand everything I did turned into peace, and everyone benefited greatly—especially my daughter.

Take a trip with me.

I want to show you how even when I was dealt a bad hand, I could change the narrative. A real person with a really challenging story can achieve peace and harmony in co-parenting. One day, I looked up and things were far better than I could have even envisioned, and I know that you can achieve that too. Of course, some will be harder than others, and some might not care that much about bettering themselves. But I know in my heart if you can understand this co-parenting philosophy and tie it together, at bare minimum, even if the other parent might not be on board, you can find solace in your attempts.

I've always been a person to share something I see as beneficial. I'm not a gatekeeper to information, and I don't want to be the only person who could benefit from something. When I finally realized I had peace within, I had to share my discovery and quantify every step of the process. I want to impact positively on the world in some way. Solving a prevalent problem, especially in the United States, was important to me. I didn't know writing a book was the vehicle, and I didn't think I was capable of it, but this book is here now—my perspective through my I cannot speak for my daughter's mother. I can only speak from my point of view. Maybe she can write something in the future about her perspective, but I'll start here with what I went through emotionally and my determination to help my daughter come out the winner. There are so many children in this world who suffer in tumultuous divorces. Their parents' disagreements shouldn't be theirs to bear. They don't the fights over stupid shit.

This philosophy will provide clarity and the confidence for peace—which is actually attainable. Although I will give you the map, you still have to climb the mountain. This book is primarily a perspective, coaching your situation. You cannot dictate what the other team is gonna do, but you learn their tendencies. With learning their tendencies, you can put together a game plan to strategically approach your situation in a way that reaps positive results. I see it as a trickle-down effect, and I guarantee that your light will shine. Play to your strengths, but most importantly, know your weaknesses and triggers. Know your "opponent" (the other parent) strengths, weaknesses, and triggers as well.

As you put together the main points in this book, things will change right before your eyes. Sometimes you have to take a few losses in order to win big for your child(ren). When solutions and results are your unwavering focuses, you are instantly solving half of the problem.

"The happiness of your life depends upon the quality of your thoughts." – Marcus Aurelius

CHAPTER 1

The Child Comes First, No Matter What

For parents who do not have a healthy, working co-parenting relationship, the child(ren) get put on the backburner to make room for egos and emotions. Children should not absorb our problems regardless of how difficult a breakup can be. Love and affection must be present to prevent damage from arising.

In a divorce or separation, the priority should always be the children. This is not to say that the parent's needs are not important, but rather that the children are more vulnerable and require more support during this time of upheaval. Parents must work together to create a parenting plan that meets the whole family's needs. This plan should include a schedule for custody and visitation, as well as a communication and conflict resolution method. By putting the children first, the parents can help ease the transition and provide them stability during difficult times.

To me, it's really simple, but looking back, I wanted a child more than I wanted to be a husband. I wanted the unconditional love and support that I didn't always have from my parents. Even though my granny was everything to me and as close as we were, I still yearned for my parent's love and acceptance. In my mind, having a child would do that for me. And I was right—my daughter was the fulfillment and happiness I sought my whole life. But in hindsight, my focus should have been on being happy with my wife—who would have borne my children. This is why putting my child first is always easy for me—as easy as my goal was to have a child and be the father I thought my father should've been.

My story will be different from a lot of people. I do realize some people did not *want* to have a child. Whatever the case may be, a child is still the responsibility of the man and woman who conceive it.

We often see children used as bargaining chips between the mother and father. Every decision after having kids, though, should be made after asking: "How are my actions affecting my child?" Is this decision in the best interest of my children? Is my ego dictating my actions? Am I letting emotions take over?

My epiphany came when looking into my daughter's eyes during my argument with her mother. It was pure horror. It pierced my soul as if I went back in time and felt the same emotions of being a three- or four-year-old child listening to my mother yell and scream. This was a feeling I never wanted to experience again and certainly not recreate it and subject my daughter to it. At that moment, I dropped the ball and instantly felt so horrible.

When children are used as bargaining chips between the mother and father in a divorce, the child is seen as an object that can be used to get what the parent wants from the other parent. This is not only emotionally damaging to the child, but it can also lead to legal problems. When a divorce is finalized, the parents must agree on who will have custody of the child (and when, if dual). If one parent uses the child as a bargaining chip, it can create a situation where the other parent feels they have no choice but to agree to whatever terms are offered. This can hurt the relationship between the parents and the child. Both parents need to be able to put their differences aside to make decisions in the best interest of the child.

I've seen numerous times when the mother will not let the father see his kids because of some emotionally charged disagreement. It could be because the father has officially moved on and gotten into a new relationship. It could be not enough child support or even none at all. Fathers need to take care of their responsibilities, but there could be more to the story. And it's not just the mothers—fathers sometimes act irrationally out of emotions too. Most of the time, the men I've noticed act out in post-divorce co-parenting is because they want that person back or it's hurting them to see her with someone else.

I've seen stories where men shut down because they were required to pay child support. The circumstances aside, whether it's justified or not, the child shouldn't have to suffer in the relationship. It's crazy how people think they hurt the other parent when the child suffers the most. The child comes first, so no matter how mad you are at the other parent. Think about how your child adores them.

My daughter adores her mother, so I can never talk badly about her or engage in unnecessary verbal back-and-forth around her. If my child comes first, everything she truly cares about needs to be something I care about, or at the very least consider. Do we have disagreements that need to be hashed out? All the time. But it doesn't always have to be a soap opera.

There are certainly situations wherein you need to keep the child from the other parent. Although I always adored my mother and love her to this day, may God rest her soul, it would've been a detriment if I had been with her as a child. I know for a fact I would be a different person if I were still here at all. I would've been in a different environment and probably seen things a child should never see. I can't say I know what it's like living with a parent on drugs. But I knew kids my age who did and some are no longer with us. For this reason, I hold my Granny in the highest regard of all humans that ever lived because she created a safe environment and nurturing space for me. And I know she's watching from above and pleased with how I'm carrying on her legacy.

Maybe my mother thought about me first because she never fought for me back nor fought to see me while she was deep in her addiction. Maybe that statement is another ploy to ease my heart and give my mind some rest. After all this, I don't have a single ounce of resentment toward my mother. Even though the drugs took her away from me at an early age and ultimately took her life on my thirty-first, I still miss her and love her deeply. I'm in my forties now, and although I never really knew her, I still think of the "what-if." Millions of scenarios pop into my head, but I never thought her absence was *not* in my best interest.

Let me give a little backstory because there is certainly a reason I'm super passionate about helping parents find peace in co-parenting. We have to search deep within to find out what drives people to give their all to something. I love my parents to death despite their shortcomings. My mother is no longer here with us, but my father is. I was even hesitant to write this because my father is still alive and we are in a great space. But I could not give you my truths and vulnerability without including him. Ultimately, my experience made me a better person. Empathy leads me not to excuse their actions and ways but to understand.

My father told me he didn't know my mother was pregnant with me until he saw my mother on Crenshaw, already seven months pregnant. Damn, I could imagine without him elaborating that there was already turmoil before I took my first breath.

I believe my earliest memory of my parents was the breakup argument (or what seemed to be that). This is as far as I remember because they were in different houses after that argument. My mom and I were living in Inglewood with some guy. But I also remember being in the same house during that argument with my dad. It had two rooms, and I still didn't understand at the time. I was a quiet, reserved kid who didn't ask questions and just went with the flow. Shortly after, I didn't return to my dad's house where the argument happened. There was my example of co-parenting. There was nothing I could get from that as an example of how to work together for the greater good of the child.

During this period with my mom, maybe a year or two, I remember going places with her and seeing her pick up little sandwich bags full of green stuff. (I know what that green stuff is now.) Two places we used to frequent were in "the jungles" across the street from HillCrest Elementary and an apartment on Adams and Arlington. This was the early eighties, so I'm not incriminating anyone. I have very distinct memories of this period. Not one memory of going to the park or doing anything a child would see as "fun." These memories don't have anything to do with anything. They are neither good nor bad. These memories are so cut-and-dry that I don't have any emotion, and I hate that it's that way. But let me continue because every memory made me want more for my life.

During this short time with my mom, I remember her waking up early and making me drink some milk and orange juice with whatever breakfast I had, and I wouldn't say I liked it. I was dropped off at my grandmother's house, and my mother went to work.

I remember the guy we were staying with—I think his name was Larry—always watching Lakers games and having people over. Maybe that's why I've never been a Lakers fan. I don't ever remember talking to him or him ever talking to me. He was a tall, dark-skinned dude that reminded me of Tommy "The Hitman" Hearn. I also remember incense always lit in the house. I know why now, but I do still like the aroma.

In this same short period, I do not remember my dad. He was around—just not around *me*. I don't remember any interactions or exchanges with my parents at this particular time. There are some things I can't recollect of them. So on the personal level in my actual life, there was no co-parenting. It was non-existent.

After that period, one day I was at Granny's house where my dad was also living, and that was it for my mom. The arrangement changed in an instant. Looking back at it, the arrangement needed to change. I can imagine that the loyalty to the dominant drug at the time. Her responsibility as my primary caretaker was too much. I can't say who made that executive decision for me to be at my Granny's house, but I always gave my Granny the credit because she took care of me like I was her own. That forged a special bond until her dying days.

It was years until I saw my mother again. The only time my dad discussed my mom was when I was about nine. A commercial was talking about getting money from child support if the other parent was absent. Since he always complained about how he didn't have it, I suggested he call the number on the screen and get some of this free money. He responded,

"You want me to take money out of your mother's pocket?"

I instantly said "No," and felt bad for even suggesting that.

Even though I hadn't seen my mother in years and didn't fully understand the extent of her condition, I knew she wasn't in a favorable position. That day was when I saw the empathy my father carried for her. She even had full medical and dental insurance because he never officially divorced her.

This was the eighties in Los Angeles at the heart of a crack cocaine epidemic. Unfortunately, my mother was a casualty of war. I call it a war because it was biological warfare on black people in America's inner cities. Crack almost wiped out the black community. I witnessed firsthand how it destroyed the black family...my family. There was a crack house next door to me when I was little. Traffic all day long, but they never messed with me. And I was from that generation of kids outside every day. I was and needed to be outside, so I was always outside. Nobody messed with me or tried to influence me greatly, and my Granny watched me like a hawk. People around the neighborhood would say they don't mess with Mrs. Hurston's grandkids or it would be a problem.

Even though the drugs and illegal activity destroyed our communities, ironically, Lamborghinis and Mercedes used to roll up and down my street. I used to look up to those guys, not knowing how they damaged our community and were the reason I didn't see my mother. This is something I didn't realize until later on in life.

My father worked the graveyard shift. That meant he rested during the day and didn't have the time or energy for me. Not having my mother around was more of a lesson than anything. I knew the feelings I had, and I would never subject my children to them. I would never subject my children to neglect no matter what. When I see the disappointment and hurt in my princess' eyes that day, it brought me back to a place I'd once known. It brought me back to the promise that I made to myself as I was possibly feeling the same emotions that she felt in that moment. My mission now was clear. I knew it would not be easy, but nothing was gonna stop me from completing my mission of creating a safe and peaceful place for my princess to thrive in.

I had to figure it out just like everyone else. It's the relationship with my daughter that pushed me and guided me along this path. I had it rough emotionally growing up. I know exactly how it felt to go without harmony, and I vowed not to let my daughter feel any of that. More important was the obligation I had to myself. I realized that I couldn't count on anyone else to grant me happiness. No one on this planet will decide whether I have peace of mind or chaos of the mind. I can control that with my perspective. The day I chose to approach co-parenting differently was the day that everything and everyone around me benefitted.

So think about it: if we are putting our children first, we don't let others dictate how we react, and we don't take our frustrations out on our kids. We should think about them, careful not to put them in compromising positions, and always keep them in safe spaces.

If you are dealing with someone who does not create a safe space for your child or you feel like you are not in the right environment, by all means, do what you have to do. Of course, if you are the parent not in the ideal situation for the child, then I hope you are doing all you can to change and/or advocate for your child.

Children are not accountable for the mistakes of their parents or the bad decisions they have made, but they often feel guilty about their breakups.

All separations and break-ups affect children. This is something we have to keep in mind at all times. This was the first thing that I thought about during mine. My mind was all over the place trying to figure this out. Parents not sharing the same house with them is a monumental change in life. Prior to separation, they only knew about living with both parents. The child kept them both glued to the cradle from birth, attending to their calls. But now, all of a sudden, they are left seeing only one at a time. Everything you do should be through the lens of creating a healthy, safe, and secure life for our kids.

"If you are distressed by anything external, the pain is not due to the thing itself but to your estimate of it, and this you have the power to revoke at any moment." – Epictetus

CHAPTER 2

Is Arguing Even Worth It?

After only a few times, I felt something needed to change. I pride myself on not having to come out of my character. Arguing has never been a part of my character unless I'm talking about sports, and even then, I'll rarely argue about sports nowadays.

Engaging in healthy debates and discussions can be a productive way to exchange ideas, challenge perspectives, and promote intellectual growth. However, when arguing becomes a destructive habit that permeates daily interactions and relationships, it can have detrimental effects on personal connections.

Constant arguing can create a hostile and tense environment, leading to increased stress, frustration, and emotional exhaustion. It hampers effective communication and hinders the development of trust and mutual understanding within relationships. When arguments become frequent and intense, they can erode the emotional bond between individuals and contribute to a sense of disconnection.

Constant arguing often focuses on "winning" or being right rather than seeking understanding or finding common ground. This approach can escalate conflicts, intensify divisions, and lead to a breakdown in communication. It becomes less about engaging in healthy debates and more about asserting one's dominance and/or building their ego, which can be damaging to relationships and hinder their growth. This is where I told myself something has to change; it wasn't about being right. Being right gets me nowhere.

Arguing incessantly can also prevent individuals from truly listening to one another. Talking over the other person creates more distance from the solution. When the focus is solely on making one's point or proving someone wrong, active listening and empathy suffer. This lack of genuine engagement can undermine effective communication and prevent the resolution of conflicts in a constructive manner.

To foster healthier relationships, it is important to cultivate effective communication skills, which include active listening, empathy, and respectful dialogue. This involves recognizing when arguments are becoming unproductive and learning to shift the focus toward understanding, compromise, and finding common ground. It requires a willingness to let go of the need to win or be right and instead prioritize the well-being and harmony of the relationship.

Most people don't understand how arguing in front of your child can affect them. In my opinion, arguing is solely based on ego and pride. This is something that I had to learn, and it took me until I was damn near forty. See, I'm the type that cannot switch moods quickly, so if I'm upset, it takes me a long time to get out of that funk. I realized over time, whether I'm right or wrong, if the other person is not receiving it how I want them to, it will upset me.

I'm sure some people worldwide have that same thought and mood pattern as I do. This gets you nowhere and upsets your world for days.

Now think about the children; they truly reflect your good and bad. The only difference is that they can't differentiate between what to do and what not to do. They are learning life from you. It's more of what you do versus what you say, unfortunately.

Children are constantly absorbing information from their environment, including how their parents interact with one another and handle various situations. They learn about communication, problem-solving, conflict resolution, empathy, and emotional regulation by observing the behaviors and responses of their parents. Therefore, what parents do carries more weight than what they say.

When parents consistently demonstrate positive behaviors, such as effective communication, respect, empathy, and healthy conflict resolution, children are more likely to internalize and replicate those behaviors in their own lives. Negative behaviors—such as constant arguing, disrespect, or aggression—can also be absorbed by children and manifested in their own actions and relationships.

It is crucial for parents to be aware of the impact they have on their children and strive to model positive behaviors and values. This involves being mindful of one's own actions, emotions, and reactions especially in front of children. By consistently displaying empathy, kindness, and healthy communication, parents provide a strong foundation for their children to develop these essential life skills.

Parents are human and may make mistakes or exhibit negative behaviors from time to time. When this happens, it becomes an opportunity for parents to model accountability, forgiveness, and the ability to learn from one's actions. By openly acknowledging and rectifying mistakes, parents teach children valuable lessons about taking responsibility and growing from challenging situations.

As a parent, the first thing I feel that is a detriment to the kids is if I can't control my emotions. Some arguments can be civil and even-tempered, but most are loud and boisterous. Let's be real here: the basis of an argument is both parties pleading their case. "I need you to feel what I'm feeling or see it how I see it," and this is, in most cases, irrational thinking.

I don't ever remember seeing my dad argue with anyone. Well, maybe that one time as a child. It was him and my mom, right before the split, but it wasn't too heated. He was always mild-mannered and even-tempered. I did inherit that trait. It takes a lot to "turn up" or react out of my character. So, for the most part, I operated in a controlled manner until there were times I didn't.

Looking back, I hated those times when my daughter saw me in an altered state. In her eyes, I'm a superhero who is always there when she needs me and always comes to her rescue. The way she looked at me in those times of rage, almost as if I was unrecognizable, must've been so scary for her. And to someone who gets pure joy from seeing my child genuinely happy, it's the opposite when she sees the other side of me.

We must realize that we are our kid's first "life" teachers. They mimic us more than we know it. We subliminally teach them life and how to handle situations. I notice how my princess is like me in many ways. I want her to be a better version than me. So acting out of character is not going to get me results.

Although discussion and communication are essential in co-parenting, arguing in front of children can leave a mark on them. Parents often fight without realizing that arguing in front of their children is significantly impactful. Children may be too young to understand what is happening and generate negative emotions in response to external stimuli. Later on, we may mistakenly assume they are old enough to face adult problems without this being the case. In other words, we think they have the maturity and the tools to handle the situation healthily, but in reality, they don't.

Controlling our reactions as human beings is so underrated. It's almost like a badge of honor to turn up in a situation where you feel disrespected. The crazy part is that almost one hundred percent of the time, that leads to an unsatisfying outcome. That's what I never understood—how important satisfying your ego is to people despite the lack of progress it brings.

Ego and pride versus rationale and solutions.

Let me give you an example: "I'll go to jail behind mine."

In other terms, "Disrespect my child, and I'll do something in retaliation that's going to put me in jail."

This isn't an uncommon statement for parents who are upset to make. Now think about it: you've retaliated, and now your child has lost a parent to the state prison or worse. Is this helping or hurting them more than the infliction that triggered you?

Look, I'm not saying I don't handle situations that need to be handled. But they should be handled with calculated rage. What I mean by that is putting a little thought behind whatever you intend to do. Shooting someone because they did something minor to your child would *not* be an example of calculated rage. Getting into a heated argument that leads to a physical fight in front of your child is also not an example of calculated rage. I do believe there are different ways to handle things so you don't have to take an ego hit. You just have to figure out what's the best method for you not to lose control or appear as though you have.

The tone of voice, sudden movements, and other elements of non-verbal language can be misinterpreted even by a baby. Although the content is not understood, they will hold onto those negative emotions.

Arguing in front of children will only lead to them absorbing the wrong type of relationship model. What's more, studies have found that when parents argue in front of their children, it can cause long-term damage to their mental and physical health. This is why it is essential for parents to try and avoid arguing in front of their children as much as possible.

When there is understanding between two parties, we can resolve conflicts rather than get stuck in the middle of a power struggle. We understand each other's intentions and needs, and work together to find solutions. Understanding leads to cooperation, collaboration, and problem-solving that works for everyone involved, not just one side. Disrespect compounds problems and rarely leads to positive outcomes. So if you want to solve any issue or situation in life, it's important to start by seeking understanding over disrespect. It's essential for creating powerful relationships and coming up with successful strategies!

To make sure we are operating from a place of understanding instead of disrespect, ask questions before trying to impose your will on others or expecting them to do things your way. Try to understand the other person's point of view and explain yours in return. This helps to create a mutual understanding and opens up a dialogue that can lead to positive solutions. When we understand each other, we create possibilities instead of problems. This is exactly what we want our children to see and teach them.

Although you do not always agree on everything, constantly arguing in front of the children would lead to losing authority. The little ones would begin to cry and question what each of the parents says simply because they see that the other disagrees. They would not know who to pay attention to or manipulate themselves according to the instructions given.

Lastly, frequent arguments lead to division and an expectation, real or perceived, for a child to take a "side." The children do not have to be referees or judges; they do not even have to attend the debates. Both parents must be very important to them and have a role at the same level.

"To find peace within, one must learn to let go of the things they cannot control." – Seneca

CHAPTER 3

Co-Parenting 101

I never envisioned myself in a situation where I would have to co-parent. That wasn't something that I even thought was possible. I'm not the kind of person that can hop into a relationship. When I do get in one, it's a big deal for me. With my daughter's mother, I felt like that was it for me. But the universe had other plans. We divorced. Remember my promise that I would never neglect my daughter and that she wouldn't suffer like I did growing up? Now it just got a lot harder.

I didn't have it figured out, but I now *had* to figure it out. I remember tearing up in the car because I knew I wouldn't get to see my princess every day anymore. I needed to figure out how to move out and survive and still give my daughter everything she already had and more. And to make things as normal as possible for her. Until then, I had been with or at least seen her every single day.

My baby was my priority, and that's how I maneuvered. Without compromising the man I am, I figured out how to get consistent wins. Whether we like it or not, my ex-wife and I are a team and have the shared goal to raise this child to the best of our abilities. We desire to empower her to conquer any and everything in her path.

We created a perfect co-parenting situation. I don't use the word "perfect" loosely. I'm authentic and cannot just sit here and sell you a dream. I practice everything I preach. I am passionate about helping others see the light as I once saw it. Over the course of four decades, extensive research consistently demonstrates the crucial advantages of shared parenting when it comes to child development and the adaptation process for both parents and children after separation and divorce. This holds particularly true in situations like the anticipation of a new sibling.

Co-parenting or "shared parenting" is, in essence, when both parents, whether divorced or separated, share the responsibility of raising their child, albeit with one parent typically shouldering more duties and spending more time with the child.

Just like any significant crisis, a separation sets in motion an adaptation process that encompasses various changes. These changes, however, are unique to each individual involved and influenced by personal characteristics such as their capacity to adapt to the new circumstances, past experiences, and individual traits.

Many psychologists suggest that separation initiates a grieving process triggered by the dissolution of a partnership. You cease to be a couple. Similar to any grieving process, factors like whether the loss was anticipated or sudden impact how children and the parents assimilate and the time required for healing. Nonetheless, the journey of adapting to the aftermath of a breakup is a gradual transformation, devoid of pre-established timelines, and profoundly personal.

One of the most significant benefits attributed to shared parenting is its influence on fostering secure attachments. Additionally, it impacts behavior within the school environment. Shared parenting also shapes parenting practices, such as effectively establishing boundaries and providing emotional support in both households consistently. Equally noteworthy are the effects on the emotional well-being of parents themselves. These far-reaching benefits have elevated co-parenting to a paramount position in the realm of family dynamics, surpassing outdated patterns and relational styles.

On the verge of separation or divorce, the concept of co-parenting may come up, but it's only when we step into the role of being our child's parent that we truly comprehend the challenges it brings.

To effectively navigate co-parenting, we must come to terms with the circumstances that led to the end of our marriages. It requires finding innovative ways to communicate and interact with our ex-partners, forging a new path for ourselves, all while keeping our children's well-being in mind.

The success of our parenting will play a vital role in how well we adapt to this change. A shared parenting arrangement thrives when there's a healthy relationship between the parental figures. Positive outcomes are more likely when support and cooperation prevail, while negative outcomes arise from disagreements, conflicts, and rejection. This holds true regardless of whether we're in a relationship with the other parent. Parenting, in its essence, refers solely to the relationship established by two individuals as parental figures.

Co-parenting becomes a means of establishing a collaborative parenting dynamic, even in the face of separation from the other parent.

It's important to note that co-parenting doesn't necessarily mean equal parental roles or an even distribution of time spent with the child. The emphasis is on teamwork and satisfactory agreement between both parties to address the essential needs of nourishment, protection, and the physical and emotional development of their children.

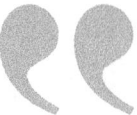

"The solution to every problem lies within our own mindset and perspective." – Zeno of Citium

CHAPTER 4

Boundaries

Boundaries in a co-parenting situation are guidelines both for their interactions with each other and for how they want to parent consistently between households. As I say a lot in this book, think about the children first. We are looking to have our children first in our minds when setting these boundaries. These are boundaries about all things related to how we parent our children, the time we spend with them, the things we expose them to, etc.

A lot of people don't think about boundaries. The idea of having to co-parent is hard enough. It's new and uncharted territory for many people. You have to worry about many things, and boundaries are the last thing on the to-do list. In my opinion, this is not one of the first tasks to get settled, but it's the most important regarding sustainability. Once you get to a healthy point in co-parenting, you can worry about boundaries. And to be clear—the sexual and emotional boundaries should've been taken care of before you got here. This chapter is what expectations and parenting methods are determined together.

This might be an issue when parents are highly involved in the child's daily life. I have always been deeply involved in every aspect of my daughter's life. This was the only thing I was worried about when my daughter's mother and I ended our relationship. As I was moving out, my only thoughts were when, where, and how I would see my baby. I was used to seeing her every day and thriving off her energy. I would be fine if I could have my daughter every day, but that wasn't realistic. This was important to me, and we needed to figure it out fast.

One of the main boundaries and expectations to set together is scheduling. After separation or divorce, things are going to be different. My example may be unrealistic for men, but I guess I'll let you make that decision.

At my job, I work four days a week and had three days off. I typically have every other weekend off. So every day I was off, I had my baby, that's how my ex-wife and I run things as I write this book. There were a few times when I went out of town, and there were times when she went out of town with Mommy, but other than that, if I was off, my baby was with me. On the days I work, I get off at night, so I don't have the luxury of picking her up every day from school. To ensure that I see her, I insist that I have her on my days off. Many of you will have better schedules than I have, so figuring that out might not be as hard. It might be even more complicated.

I partied so much in my twenties that I never felt like I was missing anything in staying in. I'm mostly an introvert, so my alone time is something I value, but becoming a father changed that. If I was off and I didn't have her a few times, I felt empty and bored. She is my peace. *I need to find a hobby!* The time is coming soon when she won't want to hang with her Da-Da all the time anymore, so that's something that I need to work on.

I like to streamline the process, which might make this all seem easy. The only difference between me and some of the issues that you might encounter is that I was already a great father before the divorce. This is something that can't be disputed, and yes, that made the process easier. For some of you, it will be just as easy. But for some of you, you may have struggled to be the parent you knew you should be. Or maybe the other parent has got a lot of flaws in that department. But people can change when they realize what's important. They will go to the end of the world for their kids, and better late than never!

For the "late" folks or "sometimes" parents, it's great that you want to be in the child's life. Every child deserves to have both of their parents around. Trust me, as a grown man, I wish my mother was straight and was around, if not all the time, at least regularly. I still get emotional thinking about how things could've been.

To the parents who want to come back, never get discouraged by the arrangements that were forced to be made in your absence. This is something you have to take accountability for. Work your way back up to a good relationship with the child. Your ultimate goal is to raise your child to be well-adjusted, emotionally healthy, and as happy as possible.

Trust has to be built back up, and I encourage you to never stop trying, even if it takes you longer than you envisioned. Your children will see that and appreciate it in the long run. If you are the parent who did all the heavy lifting with little to no help, I encourage you to be open to the resurgence. I understand how hard it will be because you may feel like "I can do it alone! I've made it this far! I like how things are!" But that is just from your point of view and has nothing to do with the child. As long as there wasn't any abuse or imminent danger presented, there shouldn't be a problem letting them come back. Who knows what could come out of it. Yes, we know you can do it alone, but let's not act like it isn't hard. So if you have the opportunity to get some much-needed help from the other parent, it definitely should be considered. Not only for your benefit but for the child as well.

I often think about how my daughter would fare in this world without me. Not passing away or never knowing me in the first place, but leaving one day and not coming back. I think about a scenario where she knew where I was within the world or even within the city. I know it would be tough on her. She would have to learn things on her own, like how a man should treat a woman etc. I went most of my childhood without seeing my mom, and she was in the same city as me. I know my relationships with women suffered because of it. Keep that in mind when the other parent is trying to make their way back in.

"True peace is not merely the absence of conflict but the presence of justice, understanding, and compassion." – Thich Nhat Hanh

CHAPTER 5

Letting Go of the Emotions That Tie

Having a child with someone is an attachment, but being emotionally tied is a different beast when co-parenting. Now I understand that overcoming this particular feat is a difficult one. This will probably be the hardest task for some people, but it's the most important step in co-parenting effectively. Although this is from my personal experience and from people I have spoken to, there are jewels for everyone. Now I've reached a point in co-parenting where I feel "next level." When I share my experience and ideas with my peers, they confirm to me that there is something I can bring to the world.

A part of life is unexplainable, and people grow apart. You can have true intentions for loving and being with someone for the rest of your life. Circumstances change, people change, some things are meant to last, and some things just have an expiration date. It is usually neither good nor bad; it is just what it is. And if you are reading this book with the intention of it bringing some peace into your life, then you've got to that point.

If you find yourself seeking peace and understanding in the midst of relationship challenges, reaching this point of introspection is a significant step. It signifies a willingness to reflect on the complexities of life and relationships and a desire to find peace within yourself.

Accepting that some things have a natural end allows us to focus on finding peace and moving forward rather than dwelling on what could have been. It's important to remember that finding peace is a personal journey and it may look different for each individual. It may involve self-reflection, seeking support from loved ones or professionals, and engaging in activities that bring solace and joy. By embracing the idea that some things are meant to be temporary, we open ourselves up to new possibilities and opportunities for growth and happiness.

At the beginning of my relationship with my daughter's mother, I had every intention of this being a forever thing. Not even God could've told me this would have been the outcome because I wouldn't have believed it. That's how serious I was about starting my family. I told my dad, "This is it," and I meant every word. Even when it started to go sour, I thought this was typical, and maybe it would get better one day, but if it didn't, this was my life. There was no way I was leaving and waking up with my daughter without me. I couldn't see a life like that. I was the one that was going to break the family curse and show that I could do it. And more importantly, give my daughter a two-parent household.

Unfortunately, some things in life are out of our control. We fight so hard to make things certain, not realizing that it may be detrimental to us. As bad as I wanted to break a generational curse, I mainly wanted to be able to see my baby every single day. She was the constant happiness in my life no matter what kind of day I had. This tied me emotionally to her mother; even though things were taking a turn, I had to try to make things work. But I had no clue how to make that situation better. And I didn't realize until later that this situation would be healthier with us apart. You can put on an act for people for only so long. Then things hit the fan. We have to be real with ourselves and figure out how to do what best serves everyone moving forward.

I've spoken to many women who tell me their men don't want anything to do with their kids. Some say it's because their men are mad at them. I wish I had a solution for parents who want nothing to do with their children. I wish I could show them how wonderful it is to see children happy and excited just because of our presence. Our acknowledgment means more than anything in this world.

A child is a separate entity from the other parent and should not be tied to your emotions toward that other parent. Just because you feel a certain way about the parent doesn't mean you have to take it out on the kids. It simply isn't fair to do so. If you claim you love your kids, do just that and do it consistently. They don't deserve to inherit a beef between you and the other parent. I don't care if the other parent is causing all the chaos. Be a stand-up individual and control what you can control, and that's how you react. Yes, it's easier said than done, but not impossible. Taking the other parent's emotions out of the equation can be hard. I know it's hard to disconnect from anyone you once loved emotionally.

Childhood trauma has made things easier for me to disconnect. Being able to disconnect so easily is a gift and a curse. Fortunately for me, it happened to jumpstart a lane to effective co-parenting. Love runs deep and time with someone runs even deeper. The hardest part of breaking up with someone you have been with for so long is implementing a new normal. Some people don't even know what life looks like without someone. The seemingly easy thing to do is just get back together, but a lot of those times, that's the wrong decision.

I understand I'm different in many ways. I needed peace by any means. I realized how important this step was for me. When I refer to "peace," I'm talking about peace from within. Peace of mind carries far more weight than anything else.

If you hold onto your feelings, that can prevent you from having a beautiful transition for yourself and for your kids. You must look out for your wellness and do what will bring you peace. I've always been a logical person, but when I went against the grain, put my pinned-up emotions to the side, and did everything beneficial for my daughter, I saw it just as that.

Yes, I want to root for my daughter's mother. I want her to be happy and successful because my daughter is with her half the time. I only want the best for my daughter, so her mother being happy is a huge deal.

It's always going to be a partnership between two parents. In healthy co-parenting situations, the two parents will be in the same place a lot of the time, supporting their children. Why create an uncomfortable atmosphere when you can be friends (or cordial) and make things good? At this point in the game, it's time to forget whatever broke things apart. Those things are in the past, and nothing will be able to rewrite history. Now is the time to write a new story that is beneficial to all parties involved.

Everyone is different when it comes to breakups. It's very common to see things go sour and end poorly. But you are still on the same team when you have a child. Teammates are the new norm, and the goal is for the child to win. As long as you live, that will be the case. Carrying emotions that hinder any harmony or progress is probably the most selfish thing. Most people do not see it that way. A lot of times, people forget a child has feelings.

One way to ensure that you let go of the emotions that could have you acting irrational is to take a step back and reflect. Self-inventory can be incredibly valuable when trying to make important decisions. By taking a step back and looking at ourselves as objectively as possible, we can identify any emotional biases or attachments that may be clouding our judgment. It's easy to get caught up in our emotions, but it's important to try and let them go to make rational decisions. Sometimes that means acknowledging and working through them, and other times it means putting them aside for the sake of clarity. No matter what, self-inventory ensures that we're fully aware of all the variables at play before making any decisions regarding your children. Take a deep breath, do some introspection, and make those decisions with confidence.

As a child, even though I was with my father during my childhood, I always felt like he resented me because of my mother. The lack of his support and encouragement stunted my growth as a person. My confidence was shot; that's something I still battle daily. In later conversations with my father, he said it was the way my grandfather treated and raised him. Maybe he should've buried his emotions toward fatherhood before attempting to parent me. I remember vividly when I did. Maybe the emotions clouded his vision when dealing with me. I know things could've been so different and much better even with my mom not in the picture. It hurts to think about it, but if I can open your eyes to not make similar mistakes, I'd like to do so

At eleven years old, I told myself I would be a better father than my dad. He used a lack of money and resources as an excuse, but money couldn't buy what I wanted. I just wanted attention, support, and encouragement.

That is the foundation of the way I parent. I consider myself living proof that you can turn things around in your family history.

"Pride brings its own trouble; ego traps us in a narrow vision. Let go of both and embrace humility for true growth." – Lao Tzu

CHAPTER 6

Shut Up and Listen

Seek to understand before being understood. This is one of the seven habits of highly effective people from the book by Stephen Covey.[1] The title is a little harsh, but I'm trying to show you how to get results, which is very important in the process. I love every single word in this book. I'm not just talking just to talk like a lot of so-called experts and gurus. This isn't based on a collegiate-level curriculum; this is based on true life experiences. And again, I do understand this is my personal experience and a system that I came up with that works for me. To be completely honest, I'm not saying anything "new." But I did bottle it up and packaged it nice and neat for you to take and roll with.

For many, this will be the make-or-break chapter. This was something I struggled with because I'm big on respect and how I'm talked to. I believe you can say all the right things but if you do it in the wrong way, still destroy the message. Let me explain: a lot of my arguments were based on tone. I feel disrespected if your tone is not how it should be when addressing me. And trust me, I still feel that way. Is it petty? Maybe, but hey, don't talk crazy to me.

---

1 Covey, Stephen R. *7 Habits Of Highly Effective People: Stephen R. Covey*. Reissue edition. London, UK: Simon & Schuster UK, 2013.

As I stated before, we can't control other people's actions, but we can control *our* actions. Many things changed when I started to be less reactive and sat back and listened. The lightbulb in my head went off, and I realized how to approach an ongoing situation to get things going in my favor.

Granted, some of you have children with some—pardon my French—fucked-up people. Some people thrive off the toxic energy and enjoy going back and forth. Some don't even know the word "accountability" or even "responsibility." Still, take a step back and listen because, at this point, it's more about your sanity than it is about theirs.

I am a solution-based person, so if we are not talking about how to fix something, I'm not engaging. Arguments are people wanting you to see and feel their side of a story. One day, I realized that arguments were pointless. Even if I was right, we would just go off on each other, and I'd be mad that she didn't see and feel the way I did. Then I'd be upset and carry an attitude, and no one benefits from that. It's a lose-lose situation for me. Somehow I had to change that to a win/win situation, but I didn't know how.

This was the hardest part for me because I hated being mad. I hated the feeling of harboring those types of feelings. It seemed to weigh me down in an uncomfortable way. If I were in a place where I could shake those feelings, I would be much better off. This is a gift and a curse for me; the gift is that I rarely get mad, but the curse is that when I do, it lingers longer than I can control. I figured I might not be able to control that part, but I could control how I reacted.

How can I use self-control to override pride? What is pride worth when you lose? Pride is the death of men in a literal and figurative sense, but it won't be my death. This does not mean being submissive or just rolling over and giving in because that would be worse. You being right doesn't win your arguments. Unless you enjoy arguments—but then this book is not for you. And if you like that toxic energy, pass it on to someone who can use it. This isn't for you, and we practice self-control over here.

When I started not reacting to everything and not trying to win the argument (a true challenge for me), things changed. First, they changed for me. Isn't this what we seek—for things to change for us? So we can have peace of mind and things become smoother in our lives?

I have found that these things and behaviors I change are for *me*, but everyone benefits from them.

The solutions I seek are for solitude and peace. You didn't even know you had the missing piece to a puzzle. The fulfillment you will receive will change your life. When I achieved what I once thought was impossible, it became the catalyst for my outlook on life and all the obstacles in it.

"To be free, let go of the chains of ego and find contentment in simplicity." – Diogenes of Sinope

CHAPTER 7

Think Like a Coach

This chapter serves as a crucial building block for the rest of your journey, laying the foundation for what's to come. It's almost as though without understanding the concepts within this chapter, you won't be able to fully grasp how I put it all together. When I really got to the point of having to figure things out, my critical thinking mind was all over the place. I so badly wanted to come up with a solution for me and get the results I thought I deserved.

Consider this section a vital cornerstone. An essential element that sets the stage for your entire journey ahead. Its significance lies in its ability to provide the fundamental understanding necessary to comprehend the intricate pieces that interweave throughout the subsequent chapters. Without grasping the concepts elucidated within this chapter, it becomes challenging to fully fathom the comprehensive framework that ties everything together.

When I reached the critical juncture of needing to unravel the complexities and find resolution, my mind, overflowing with thoughts, became a whirlwind of critical thinking. I found myself seeking answers and striving to devise a solution that would cater to my unique circumstances, earnestly yearning for the outcomes I believed I rightfully deserved.

The desire to unlock the path forward became a relentless pursuit, urging me to delve into the depths of my own cognitive processes. Amidst the chaotic stream of thoughts, I sought to harness the power of critical thinking, striving to piece together the puzzle that would illuminate the way forward. It was a journey of self-discovery, where introspection and discernment became invaluable tools in my quest for clarity.

Through this introspective journey, I gradually uncovered the inner workings of my mind and recognized the patterns that shaped my decision-making processes. This realization served as a catalyst, propelling me to challenge preconceived notions and broaden my perspectives. By embracing the power of critical thinking, I was able to navigate the intricate maze of possibilities and arrive at innovative solutions tailored to my unique circumstances.

In essence, this was the pivotal moment when I acknowledged the *importance* of really understanding the concepts of critical thinking.

The first thing I did was recognize my faults and where I came up short. This was a brand-new concept for me because I'm never at fault—*yeah, right!* "Let that pride go" is what I continually had to tell myself. This particular step took every bone out of my body to grasp. I was doing this to figure out how I could possibly turn my weaknesses into strengths. I quickly how pride made it hard to admit when I was wrong. This pride prevented me from having healthy and constructive conversations with her because the second I felt a disrespected I shut down which in turn created more of a barrier.

To let go of pride, I admitted aloud when I had done something wrong and listened without interruption when she spoke. This created an atmosphere of mutual respect and understanding that permitted meaningful conversations about our daughter.

Embracing the necessity of shedding my pride became a pivotal step in my personal growth. Realizing that it had been a hindrance, I set out on a path to cultivate humility and create a positive shift in my interactions. One of the key aspects was acknowledging my mistakes and taking responsibility for them, without shying away from accountability. By doing so, I aimed to foster an environment of open communication and genuine understanding.

In my pursuit of humility, I focused on actively listening, particularly when she expressed her thoughts and concerns. I recognized the significance of granting her uninterrupted space to share her perspective, allowing her words to flow freely and genuinely absorb their meaning. By wholeheartedly meditating on her words, I aimed to convey my respect for her and validate her feelings.

These exchanges went beyond surface-level discussions, delving into the depths of our shared responsibilities and desires for our child's well-being. This is where thinking like a coach comes into play. I realized that no amount or volume of arguing was going to change anyone. I made a conscious decision to redirect my energy toward a more productive approach—focusing on achieving tangible results and uncovering viable solutions.

In this transformative shift, I observed a remarkable transition within myself. Gone were the days of engaging in endless back-and-forth discussions, tirelessly striving to make her see things from my perspective. Instead, I embraced a simpler, yet immensely powerful mantra: "Let's find a solution."

Rather than getting entangled in fruitless debates, I shifted the narrative toward collaborative problem-solving. By acknowledging the importance of finding common ground, I redirected our conversations toward a shared goal—the actionable solutions.

Through the lens of a coach, I began to foster an atmosphere of open-mindedness and constructive dialogue. Instead of dwelling on our differences, I focused on the possibilities. Each conversation became an opportunity to explore potential resolutions, seeking pathways that yielded the desired outcomes for both parties.

This subtle but powerful change in mindset not only diffused tension but also created an environment conducive to collaboration and progress.

When you are playing an opponent, they're not going to run the plays that you want them to run just because you think they should run them. Coaches have a more intricate process of creating a game plan. One of my closest friends (and frat bro) Ron "Coach White" is someone I talk to often. And sometimes I'm amazed at the plays he breaks down for me. I'd often think, "Wow, I would've never seen that." It makes so much sense, and with some of his schemes, you see how it covers the whole football field. You can see how his critical thinking is a well-oiled machine.

So I started kind of looking at co-parenting that way. The only difference when using this in co-parenting is that no one loses. Everyone wins. Let me run plays that can get me first downs (solutions). You can't predict what the other team is running, and that's why coaches watch film and pick up on tendencies. In this case, you must know and understand the other parents' strengths and weaknesses and play to that to get results not to prevent a win for them but to create a win for both.

For example, my weakness was blowing up every time I felt remotely disrespected. There were many instances where I felt disrespected. What I did realize is that most of those were not her intentions. A system in my head translated her actions or words into "disrespect." Am I really being disrespected, or do I just feel disrespected?

That became the first question I asked myself (and still do). The consequences would only make me feel a certain way. I know now that those were never her intentions, and I took them personally, which created a tension while she had no clue why I was upset. The new me would give it some time, not take everything so personally, and talk it out. I would bottle so many things up, and for me, that's not the way to get results.

Understanding the tendencies of other parents can be a valuable tool for self-discovery. Often, it is our own reactions that amplify and escalate challenging situations. However, when I consciously changed my response, everything began to shift in remarkable ways. It was as if I stumbled upon a newfound state of tranquility, a level of peace I hadn't realized was within reach.

When confronted with situations that would have previously triggered feelings of disrespect and a reaction, I consciously chose not to let my emotions take control. Instead, I responded in a manner that nurtured my inner peace.

It was unnecessary to engage in a tit-for-tat battle, trying to combat fire with fire. In fact, in retrospect, the thought of such an approach seems crazy to me. Instead, I realized that by focusing on finding solutions, I could easily extinguish the flames of conflict. It became evident that the path to achieving consistent wins—peace and harmony—lie in changing my approach.

By letting go of the instinctive need to fight back, I opened myself up to new possibilities. I began seeking resolutions with a clear mind, focusing on productive communication rather than escalating confrontations. This new approach not only diffused tension but allowed for constructive dialogue, paving the way for sustained harmony.

Recognizing and understanding the tendencies of other parents can serve as a catalyst for self-reflection and personal growth. By changing our reactions, refusing to let pride take the reins, and adopting a solution-oriented mindset, we can attain a level of peace that seemed elusive before.

Instead of fueling conflict, we can transform our approach, building a foundation rooted in tranquility and nurturing fruitful relationships.

Therapy also played a significant role in my journey of self-discovery, and I owe a great deal of credit to my therapist. In my eyes, she's the GOAT (greatest of all time). It was through therapy that I began to unravel the inner conflicts plaguing me since childhood. Childhood trauma, I learned, has a way of distorting our perceptions and shaping our experiences. To gain a deeper understanding of myself, I had to step outside of my own perspective.

Thinking like a coach helped in this too. It enabled me to shift my outlook to shed light on the reasons behind my actions and behaviors. Through therapy, I embarked on a transformative exploration of who I truly was and the underlying causes that influenced my choices.

Remember when I mentioned my struggle with lingering anger? It was a sentiment that gripped me, often persisting for days on end. However, through therapy, I realized I had been employing anger as a defense mechanism, a shield born out of deep-seated childhood fears.

Therapy acted as a guiding light, illuminating the hidden recesses of my psyche. It allowed me to unearth the roots of my emotional responses, uncovering the connection between past traumas and present behaviors.

With the guidance of a skilled therapist, I was able to confront and process the fears and traumas from my past. This transformative process gave me the tools to challenge and reframe my thoughts, ultimately leading to personal growth and a healthier sense of self. By understanding the inner wars I had been battling, I gained the ability to choose a different path, one rooted in self-awareness and healing.

Therapy provided the space for introspection and self-reflection. It allowed me to peel back the layers, revealing the profound impact of childhood experiences on my present-day life. Armed with this newfound understanding, I could work toward releasing old defense mechanisms and embrace healthier coping strategies.

Within the safe and supportive environment of therapy, I felt safe to unravel the complexities of my emotions, thoughts, and behaviors. This is accessible to everyone who participates, even if it takes trying out a few therapists before the right fit.

Through this process of self-discovery, therapy helps individuals shine a light on aspects of themselves that may have remained hidden or obscured. It provides a space for honest reflection, encouraging us to delve into their past experiences, childhood upbringing, and the various factors that have shaped their identity. It allows us to gain a deeper understanding of who we are and why we behave in certain ways.

Unearthing buried emotions is another crucial aspect of therapy's role in self-discovery. Often, individuals may have repressed or overlooked their emotions due to various reasons, such as societal expectations, past traumas, or defense mechanisms. Therapy provides a supportive and non-judgmental space for individuals to explore these emotions, giving them the opportunity to process and integrate them into their lives. By reconnecting with their emotions, individuals can develop a greater sense of self-awareness and emotional intelligence.

Furthermore, therapy helps individuals identify subconscious patterns that may be influencing their lives. These patterns may stem from early experiences or learned behaviors that have become deeply ingrained. With the guidance of a therapist, individuals can make conscious choices to break free from unhelpful patterns and develop healthier ways of thinking and behaving.

Ultimately, the journey of self-discovery in therapy empowers individuals to live a more authentic and fulfilling life. By gaining clarity about their values, desires, strengths, and areas for growth, individuals can align their actions and decisions with their true selves.

Therapy serves as a catalyst for personal growth and development. It provides a nurturing environment where individuals can work on self-improvement, overcome challenges, and build resilience. A skilled therapist helps clients identify and address limiting beliefs, negative thought patterns, and self-defeating behaviors that may be hindering their progress. By challenging these obstacles and providing guidance, therapy assists individuals in cultivating healthier coping mechanisms, enhancing self-esteem, and fostering personal growth. I honestly didn't think any of that was possible until I saw it with my own eyes. My therapist literally changed my life. She might be the GOAT.

Emotional well-being has far-reaching benefits for every part of our health. Many individuals, myself included, carry emotional wounds from past experiences that can deeply affect our physical health, mental health, and spiritual health. Therapy serves as a valuable resource for healing these wounds, processing emotions, and cultivating constructive ways to navigate the challenges that arise.

One of the key aspects of therapy is the establishment of a trusting and empathetic therapeutic relationship. Within this relationship, individuals feel safe and supported to express their feelings openly without fear of judgment or criticism. This safe space allows for the exploration of emotions that may have been suppressed or overlooked, enabling individuals to gain a deeper understanding of their emotional landscape.

Through therapy, individuals can develop insights into their emotional responses and patterns. By exploring the roots of these emotions, whether they stem from past experiences, relationships, or internal dynamics, individuals can begin to unravel the layers of their emotional landscape. Therapists provide guidance and support in helping individuals recognize and make sense of their emotions, empowering them to develop healthier coping strategies and emotional regulation techniques.

Moreover, therapy equips individuals with the tools and skills to navigate life's ups and downs more effectively. Therapists work collaboratively with individuals to identify and challenge unhelpful thought patterns and behaviors that contribute to emotional distress. They help individuals develop practical strategies for emotional regulation, stress management, and self-care, fostering resilience and enhancing emotional well-being.

It's worth noting that therapy is a resource that can be beneficial for anyone, whether they are currently facing significant challenges or not. The tools are helpful for when something inevitably does come up.

Therapy provides a transformative space for emotional healing and growth. It offers individuals the opportunity to process and heal emotional wounds, gain insights into their emotional responses, and develop effective strategies for emotional well-being. By embracing therapy as a valuable tool, individuals can cultivate greater self-understanding, enhance their emotional resilience, and ultimately lead more fulfilling lives.

"The more you let go of attachments and desires, the lighter your heart becomes, allowing true peace to enter." – Confucius

CHAPTER 8

The Impact of the Breakup on You

In the challenging circumstances of a marriage breaking down or the breakup of a long-term relationship, embracing humility is an invaluable tool for both partners. Humility, in this context, doesn't entail surrendering or neglecting one's own needs, but rather recognizing that there are always multiple perspectives to consider and striving to understand each other's point of view. It involves setting aside preconceived notions and engaging in open and honest conversations that are free from blame or criticism.

By embracing humility, both partners create a foundation for effective communication and conflict resolution. Instead of approaching discussions with a defensive or combative mindset, humility allows for a more receptive and empathetic approach. It encourages active listening and genuine curiosity about each other's experiences and emotions.

Acknowledging that there are two sides to every story fosters a sense of mutual respect and understanding. Each partner recognizes that their own perspective is not the sole truth, and there is value in hearing the other person's viewpoint. This willingness to understand and empathize can open the door to finding common ground and working toward a resolution that meets both partners' needs.

Humility also involves taking responsibility for one's own actions and contributions to the relationship dynamics. It means being willing to acknowledge and reflect upon any mistakes or shortcomings. This self-reflection paves the way for personal growth and the development of healthier behavior.

Moreover, practicing humility in difficult relationship situations allows for the creation of a safe and non-judgmental space for open dialogue. By setting aside blame and criticism, both partners can express their feelings, concerns, and needs more effectively. This leads to greater understanding and more constructive solutions for the underlying issues.

Following a separation, it's normal to experience a sense of chaos and disorientation, often leaving one feeling lost. However, it is crucial to gather the strength to embark on a new chapter and move forward, pursuing personal, professional, and social aspirations. This journey of moving forward requires emotional resilience.

One of the most challenging tasks during this process is letting go of the past and the reasons why things may have turned sour. It may be difficult, but it is essential to shift the focus toward finding solutions. Acknowledge that dwelling on the past can only hinder progress. This is not to dismiss any issues with the other parent, but accepting that things didn't go as planned is the first step toward embracing the desire for self-improvement and finding purpose in life.

In this transformative phase, setting new goals becomes paramount. By focusing on personal growth and setting meaningful objectives, you can chart a new course for yourself. Identify what you want to achieve and pursue those aspirations to foster a sense of direction and fulfillment. Embracing the idea of self-improvement allows you to channel your energy into positive endeavors and find purpose in your journey.

Helpful feedback (and being open to it) is another crucial element in the process of moving forward. Seeking feedback from trusted sources like friends, family, or even professionals can offer valuable insights and guidance. Feedback can provide fresh perspectives and help you gain self-awareness, allowing for continued personal growth and improvement.

It's important to acknowledge that the transitions and stress you may experience during this period are often self-inflicted. While it's natural to feel overwhelmed, taking ownership of your emotions and mindset can empower you to navigate the challenges with resilience. By focusing on solutions, embracing the desire for self-improvement, setting new goals, and seeking feedback, you can cultivate the emotional strength and resilience needed to move forward in a positive and purposeful way.

Remember, this journey of moving forward is unique to you, and it may take time. Be patient with yourself, practice self-compassion, and celebrate each small step forward along the way.

During the emotional separation phase, individuals may experience a sense of disillusionment, disappointment, and disconnection from their significant other. This phase often involves a realization that expectations within the marriage have not been met, leading to feelings of anxiety, alienation, and confusion. It can be a challenging and distressing period as individuals grapple with the realization that the marriage may be coming to an end. This is exactly how I felt at the time of my separation. I just started thinking and feeling a way coming from my own point of view. My thoughts were racing through my mind about everything I felt she did wrong. Not once in this time period did I think about her perspective.

When parents decide to divorce or separate, the effects on their relationship with their children can be profound. As the parent-child dynamic shifts, often times, a child will experience a range of emotions such as sadness, anger, confusion, and guilt. It is important for both parents to take responsibility in helping their children adjust to these changes.

This was the most terrifying part for me because my princess was everything to me. I was so used to seeing her every day. I had absolutely no idea how I would manage at first because my work schedule was so unorthodox. To be completely honest, this was the hardest part for me because I needed just as much if not more than she needed me. It may sound crazy, but she was the calm and peace in my life.

It was probably harder on me than it was for her. Even though I had my daughter three to four days a week and every single "off" day, there were nights where I missed her dearly. I had already constructed my life around my baby. When you would see me, you would see her; bachelor life was not something that I wanted to go back to, but I had to figure it out.

Some of you are like me and may have had or are still having a hard time adjusting to the new "norm." This is another reason why you have to do everything in your control to make things manageable in your co-parenting to work out these schedules and transitions.

After a separation, the world may feel chaotic and disorienting, and it's common to experience a sense of being lost. However, it's crucial to find the strength to begin anew and move forward with personal, professional, and social aspirations, which requires emotional resilience.

Feedback provides insights into our strengths and weaknesses, allowing us to learn and make positive changes. Receiving feedback from others, such as friends, family, or mentors, can help us gain different perspectives and uncover blind spots. This is something that I learned later on but wish I sought after earlier. I actually stumbled onto it by trial and error. Then it hit me like a brick, but if I had someone school me beforehand, it would have saved me years.

It's important to approach feedback with an open mind and a willingness to grow. Constructive criticism, though it may be challenging to hear, can offer valuable guidance on areas where we can improve. By embracing feedback and using it as a catalyst for self-reflection, we can make meaningful changes and continue evolving as individuals.

Additionally, self-reflection is a powerful tool for self-discovery and personal development. Taking time to introspect and understand our thoughts, feelings, and motivations allows us to gain clarity and make choices aligned with our values and aspirations. Self-reflection can be achieved through practices like journaling, meditation, or simply taking quiet moments to contemplate. I was at my breaking point when my daughter looked at me like she didn't know me after an argument with her mother. I knew then that I had to look within for the answers and reflect on what I can do immediately to help me through this process.

Remember, the journey of finding oneself after a separation is unique to each individual. It requires patience, self-compassion, and a commitment to personal growth. Embrace feedback, engage in self-reflection, and stay open to new experiences. Through this process, you can discover a renewed sense of purpose, find inner strength, and create a fulfilling life for yourself.

Often, a separation or breakup happens when one person disagrees or feels dissatisfied with the other, the relationship, or even themselves. In such moments, individuals reflect on their relationship and contemplate the decision they need to make. During this period, the discontentment they feel can manifest in unusual attitudes and behaviors.

When one party is not prepared for the breakup, they may react differently, exhibiting denial or attempting to salvage the relationship due to the emotional attachment or time invested. This can lead to feelings of anger and frustration. As a result, both individuals may engage in arguments, make excuses, place blame on each other, and express frustration even over trivial matters. I realized that I was blaming her for everything without taking any accountability for things I could have done better. I ultimately knew it was the end, but at the time, I had to attach the blame on something, and unfortunately, I put it on her because I was embarrassed for not keeping the family together, and more so not keeping my "two-parent household" promise to my daughter.

The process of separating a couple involves a sudden disruption of the way of life that had been established until that point. It requires the reorganization of one's own life and the rebuilding of social and family relationships.

The psychological effects of a couple breakup can be profound, extending beyond the immediate individuals involved to impact the family unit as a whole. The family, as the primary group, plays a crucial role in shaping the identities, values, and beliefs of its members, particularly through intimate and close interactions between parents and children.

When a couple separates, the stability and familiarity that the family unit once provided becomes disrupted. This disruption can have significant psychological consequences, especially for children who rely on the family as their identity matrix. The breakup may challenge their sense of self, self-esteem, and understanding of relationships. The values, beliefs, and customs they have internalized from their family may need to be reevaluated or readjusted.

The family's function as a source of security and emotional refuge also undergoes a transformation. The breakup introduces change, uncertainty, and potentially conflicting emotions within the family dynamic. The sense of security that the family once provided may be compromised, leaving individuals to grapple with feelings of instability and vulnerability.

For adults, the psychological effects of a couple breakup can manifest in various ways. They may experience grief, loss, and a range of other emotions like sadness, anger, and confusion. The breakup may challenge their own sense of identity and self-esteem, leading to introspection and a reevaluation of personal values and goals.

It is important to acknowledge that the psychological effects of a couple's breakup can vary widely depending on individual circumstances and coping mechanisms. Some individuals may exhibit resilience and adaptability while others more intensely with the emotional aftermath.

Seeking support both inside and outside the family can significantly help with navigating the breakup mentally. Professional counseling can provide a safe space for individuals to process their emotions to develop healthy coping strategies. Support from friends or support groups can also offer comfort and validation during this challenging time.

As the family undergoes transformation and individuals navigate the psychological effects of the breakup, it is important to recognize that healing and growth are possible. By embracing self-reflection, seeking support, and engaging in healthy coping mechanisms, individuals can find resilience and establish a new sense of stability and well-being in their post-breakup lives.

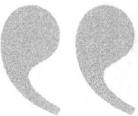

"The source of our suffering lies in our expectations. Let go of them and you will find serenity." – Gautama Buddha

CHAPTER 9

Modeling Appropriate Behavior

One therapy session, my therapist used a helpful label for our discussion: appropriate model behavior (MAB). I heard this, then a light bulb went off in my head. That phrase I was looking for that described what I've been doing the last two years that put everything together.

Every single principle I've shared, I've implemented. But none of these principles would've worked without plugging the machine into the power source to give it life. Now some of you might ask what I mean by this. It's like doing all this work building a car but not having gas (or for you electric vehicle people, a charge). How effective is the car now with nothing to fuel it from point A to point B? You've done all this great work, but ultimately, you will not go anywhere.

MAB means acting and behaving as you want the other parent to act and conduct themselves. For the sake of this book, that's my definition, but it can be used in other aspects of life. This takes a deep dive and may expect some of you to dig deeper than ever. It may take you so far out of your comfort zone that you may seem unrecognizable to yourself.

The best way to get people to conform is to model the behavior you want to see. If you want people to be on time, be on time yourself. If you want people to be respectful, be respectful yourself. People are more likely to conform to your behavior if they respect you and see you as a role model. Of course, there will always be people who don't want to conform to your behavior no matter what you do. In those cases, it's important to remember that you can't force someone to change their behavior. All you can do is lead by example and hope they eventually come around.

Toxic is some of you guys' love language. Not to kick anyone while they are down, but you must acknowledge that. You must understand how some of your actions and reactions play in a dysfunctional co-parenting situation. I use the word "toxic" far broader than how its colloquial definition in modern culture. To me, it's any and everything that is done to contribute to low-level co-parenting.

Many people find themselves in the position of co-parenting after a divorce or breakup. While it is possible to co-parent effectively, it can be challenging. One of the biggest challenges is dealing with an ex-partner who is unwilling or unable to cooperate. This can result in a situation where one parent constantly has to adjust their actions and reactions to try to maintain some semblance of order.

First, remember that you are not alone. There are many resources available to help you navigate these waters. You will need to be patient and understand that it may take some time to find a solution that works for everyone involved, but with perseverance and understanding, it is possible to create a healthy co-parenting relationship.

We hear the saying "keep that same energy" a lot, or phrases that may have a similar meaning—mostly used to describe replicating the toxic behavior. This is exactly what you should *not* do. Doing this will keep you in a deplorable situation. Two wrongs don't make a right, and as cliché as that is, it's never been so relevant. I've never seen that type of situation thrive, and it logically doesn't make sense.

When I started my journey, fortunately for me, wanting my daughter to see me in another light propelled me into MAB. Before I knew the outcome, I was doing it for my daughter.

It's not just kids who need to be taught how to behave. Parents need modeling too! Just like children learn by observing and imitating the behavior of adults, parents can learn how to co-parent effectively by observing and imitating the behavior of other effective co-parents. This doesn't mean that you have to go out and find another couple to serve as your role models (although that could be a great idea!). You can learn a lot by observing other families, reading books or articles about co-parenting, or watching TV shows or movies portraying healthy family dynamics.

Modeling appropriate behavior helps all three areas of the co-parent triangle. But even before my daughter and her mother, it benefited me the most. One would think I'm solely doing this to get the other parent to adapt, but that's not the case. Remember, I was doing this in the beginning so my daughter wouldn't see me as this unrecognizable person. MAB was not initially intended for myself or for my daughter's mother.

Now I consider myself genuine and very considerate, so operating in my truest form was not hard for me. I always take the time to think about how my actions will affect others, and I am always willing to help out however I can. I believe that being genuine and considerate are two of the most important qualities a person can have. For some of you, this will require you to dig deep and extract what we all, as human beings, can do. Your main focus in modeling appropriate behavior should be not allowing your ego and pride to take over.

Imagine it as your first professional boxing match. The athlete doesn't just go in and fight without training or they will get destroyed. Professional boxers start training months before the fight by doing the most burdensome workouts, and some of them workout all year long. Waking up before everyone else, running miles in cold weather, and most of all, being consistent. This training is done even when a guaranteed win is not promised. All the hard work may not come when we think it should, but it will come in due time.

MAB benefits the kids in more ways than one. Not only are we showing them how to deal with situations, but we are demonstrating how to be outstanding human beings. We provide a baseline for solution-based conflict resolution, always focused on getting results. It's impossible to argue our way into better solutions or get what we want out of the situation. Take a deep look into how one's thought process is. People would probably argue with me on this point, but arguing has nothing to do with finding a solution instead of having an emotional response and trying to prove a point.

When we check our emotions and consciously choose our responses, we demonstrate to our children the power of emotional regulation. By being mindful of our reactions, we show them that we can effectively manage situations rather than being controlled by them. This valuable lesson teaches them that they, too, have the capacity to influence their own circumstances.

Life is filled with unpredictable moments where outcomes may sway in different directions. Acknowledging this reality, we understand that we cannot control every situation, but we can always control how we respond to them. Taking charge of our reactions empowers us to be proactive and intentional in our original actions, leading us closer to achieving the desired results.

As our children witness us exercising emotional control, they learn that their emotions need not dictate their responses. They grasp the significance of self-regulation in problem-solving, conflict resolution, and decision-making. They observe how we handle adversity with grace and determination, providing them with a blueprint for developing resilience and adaptability.

Furthermore, by instilling the skill of emotional control in our children, we provide them with invaluable tools to navigate the complexities of life. As they continue to grow and encounter diverse situations, they can tap into their cultivated ability to regulate their emotions and manage their reactions.

This self-mastery becomes a guiding force in their lives, empowering them to maintain a strong sense of agency and take charge of their own experiences. Instead of being at the mercy of external circumstances, they develop the capacity to respond thoughtfully and purposefully.

By having a heightened awareness of their emotions and the ability to control their reactions, our children become more resilient and adaptable. My children being able make sound decisions in life is a big value to me as a parent. I'm not going to be able to be with them every moment of life, so feeling comfortable with them making decisions in the world would mean everything to me.

Through the practice of emotional regulation, our children learn that they have the power to shape their own narratives. They understand that while they may not have control over every external factor, they always have control over their internal world, their emotional state, and their chosen responses.

As they witness the positive outcomes that arise from us as parents exercising emotional control, our children develop a strong belief in their own capabilities. This belief becomes the foundation for their personal growth, allowing them to pursue their aspirations, overcome obstacles, and create meaningful connections with others.

"True wisdom lies in realizing that the path to peace is not through dominance and control but through self-mastery and understanding." – Epictetus

CHAPTER 10

Peace

At the end of this journey to effective co-parenting, the result is peace. I could technically end things there as I'm very much straight to the point. But let's look at it this way: there are some people for whom this book will not work. You may be dealing with someone who doesn't care about you or, more importantly, the child.

Could that person turn things around and be better? Sure, anything is possible. One would hope the importance of raising a child in a healthy environment encompasses every parent's soul. There are a lot of people who just don't know how. It's hard to will our way to a better situation when life hasn't given us any up-close and personal examples. But making it this far in the book shows me that you want to progress and are willing to sacrifice.

I can relate to the challenges many of you faced in not having positive examples of healthy co-parenting or a harmonious household. It can be particularly difficult to navigate such situations when we lack firsthand experience or role models to guide us. However, despite the absence of those examples, you demonstrated tremendous resilience and determination by willing yourself to find a place of peace.

Willpower, coupled with a strong desire for change and personal growth, can be a transformative force. It requires a conscious decision to break free from negative patterns and actively seek a different path. By recognizing the importance of establishing a peaceful co-parenting dynamic and a harmonious environment for yourself and your child, you took the first step toward creating a positive change.

Achieving a state of peace often involves self-reflection and introspection. It means examining our own attitudes, behaviors, and beliefs, and being open to self-improvement. It requires letting go of past hurts, forgiving ourselves and others, and embracing a mindset focused on growth, understanding, and compassion.

Creating peace in challenging circumstances also calls for setting healthy boundaries and prioritizing self-care. It means recognizing when to seek support from counselors or support groups who can provide guidance and tools for navigating co-parenting challenges.

Our willingness to embark on this journey toward peace demonstrates your strength and determination. It takes courage to break free from negative cycles and forge a new path for ourselves and our children. By consciously choosing peace, we are creating a positive legacy for future generations, showing them that it is possible to overcome adversity and build a nurturing environment.

Remember, this process is not always easy, and setbacks may occur along the way. However, with our unwavering will and commitment to finding peace, we have already proven that we possess the inner strength and resilience to overcome any future obstacles.

As you continue on your path, embrace the progress you have made and celebrate each step toward a more peaceful co-parenting relationship and household. Your journey serves as an inspiration for others who may be facing similar challenges, demonstrating that with determination, self-reflection, and a focus on growth, it is possible to create a positive and harmonious environment for yourself and your child.

Understanding that I can only control what I can control was the hardest thing to accept, especially as a hands-on father. I had to understand that not everyone sees things my way, which is tough. I have to make the best of what I can. Hard pill to swallow, but it can work out in the long run.

Know who and what you are dealing with, then know yourself. It's not as easy as it sounds. There were particular triggers that I had to realize and adjust my life to. How can I get around these triggers? Because knowing myself, once I get mad, that emotion lingers for a couple of days, and I don't like that. And it doesn't do anyone any good for me to have that feeling, and more so, I think about how it's not beneficial to my daughter.

For instance, I'm big on respect and the way I'm being talked to. If a situation is not in my favor respectfully, I adjust.

I've learned not to take things personally. When we take things personally, we internalize the words or actions of others as a reflection of our own worth or character. However, the truth is that people's behavior and reactions are often more a reflection of their own experiences, perspectives, and emotional state than a direct judgment of who we are.

Understanding this concept allows us to develop a level of emotional detachment from the opinions and actions of others. Instead of internalizing everything as a personal attack, we can choose to view situations with objectivity and empathy. We recognize that everyone is going through their own journeys and may be influenced by various factors that have nothing to do with us.

By not taking things personally, we free ourselves from the burden of unnecessary emotional distress. We become less reactive and more centered, able to respond to situations calmly and thoughtfully. This newfound perspective empowers us to approach conflicts and challenges with a level-headed mindset, seeking solutions rather than becoming entangled in personal grievances.

You can only control your reactions, right? My reactions used to have me in a funk for at least two days. But that's giving people too much control over my life. When a relationship has its expiration date, and if a child is involved, you must make good of that situation.

It doesn't always have to be a bad, bitter situation. As long as you live, there will be interactions with the other parent. Why forcibly make it harder for you, them, and the children? Now, being one hundred percent honest, some people will never experience this peace because some men and women are dirtbags and pieces of shit who don't want peace. And let's go back to your reaction. Most people reciprocate the same energy that you are getting, right? And that's a logical thing that is more common than not. But in the co-parenting situation, tell me how that's made things better for you. No, I'm serious—if giving back that same negative energy has made things better, let me know, and I'll take this book off the shelves right now.

Here's the secret: if the only thing we can control is our reactions, then do just that. Your reactions should be what you want to receive. Don't let the other person turn you into a monster and someone unrecognizable to the people who know you. (I always refer back to that time when I was unrecognizable to my daughter). This only affects our children, especially when we do things despite them. Is this the hardest thing in life? Yes, But it's a game-changer.

Here's an example, and I get emotional just thinking about it.

There was a time when I was called into the room to be the "bad cop." My daughter refused to let Mommy put her pajamas on, and Mommy was tired. I despised being a bad cop, but without force, my disciplinary presence is the game changer 95 percent of the time. This particular night was different. This night was a monumental part of how this book came about.

I cannot tell you what Mommy was feeling at the time, struggling with this toddler fighting to not get ready for bed. Maybe she was tired or maybe something happened that day that really annoyed her and for some odd reason, Mommy's attitude shifted to me, which I felt was unwarranted. The whole time we'd been parents, I felt I did all I could to alleviate Mommy's pressure. So this time, I felt I was doing that like any other. A short back-and-forth ensued, and I became angry. The bad part about it was my daughter was still resisting, which was a bad combination. I don't know what my daughter was feeling or going through, but at this time, I wasn't helping her cause either, and I didn't care.

She needed to get these pajamas on so I could return to the other room. Now, I'm man handling this little girl trying to get these pajamas on, screaming at the top of her lungs, and fighting me. My anger blocked out her screams, and I proceeded. She was a strong little girl, so it took me a minute. I finally got them on and just went into the other room.

I remember it like yesterday. I went into the living room and just sat in the dark. On top of that, I was angry at myself for taking it out on the little human I love more than anything else in this world.

I'm sitting in the dark and there is only light from the TV in the bedroom, but I see this little silhouette of a child come around the corner and walk toward me. She came in, hugged me, then walked back into the room to go to bed. This is five minutes after me manhandling her to get her pajamas on. As soon as she turned the corner to enter the room, tears flowed uncontrollably down my face. This was the first time I experienced unconditional love like that. It was hard for me to grasp but looking back at it, she taught me something. That night, I told myself I would never let anyone take me out of character like that.

I was always gentle with my baby. I never needed to be like that with her, and to this day, I never have to raise my voice with her. She never deserved that, but at that time, my reactions turned me into an unrecognizable monster. That hug after my frustration symbolized that she wanted her "Da-Da" back. She wanted her first true love back, and that night, I vowed two things. First, never take any of my frustrations out on her, and never let anyone take me out of my character or control how I react to situations.

Things didn't change automatically when I started operating in that space. They are not supposed to, but operating in control over your reactions is the beginning of peaceful existence in co-parenting and life. This is not something I always figured out, and I just didn't quit. (That was a Nipsey Hussle sound bite, but it's the truth.) And to be more honest with you, it took me about three years to get to not only peace, but to where I'm considered in every decision and even accommodated in some instances. But I sacrificed hard for this and am now reaping the fruits of my labor. I never took a night off; I never said "no" to getting my daughter, even when her mom had to work at odd times or something came up.

We don't have family nearby, so it's either me or her. I've canceled many plans for my baby, and there is not one time I chose the streets over my baby. I don't expect people to be like that in that case. There are things you want to do and places you want to go, and that's fine. We are human, and you may need an outlet or escape. The crazy part is my daughter was and still is my peace. I'm very much a "social" introvert and value my alone time. But since becoming a single father, I have required a lot less alone time and much more time with my princess. Especially when I realized I felt a lot better and less anxious when she was with me.

It's to the point where I feel like I rely on my daughter for that comfort and peace. The scary part is that at the time you will be reading this, she will be nine, and I have a few more years until she's more interested in hanging with friends instead of with dad. I need to find another hobby quickly. But ultimately, the amount of peace I have is priceless.

Acknowledgements

First, I would like to thank my daughter, Nyla Symone Hurston.

Everything changed when you were born; you absolutely gave me purpose. I get emotional even writing this because you came and completely took over my heart. You may not know this, but I made a promise to you and myself twenty years before you were even born to be a better father and the best father I can learn how to be for my children.

This book and this philosophy would not have even been a thought if I didn't keep my promise that I made when I was eleven years old. No matter the obstacle, I will always try to be everything you need me to be in a father, providing a perfect amount of balance between structure and genuine love and support. I've never been this consistent in my life. I have to mention that you make fatherhood a breeze and fun. I've witnessed you do commercials with Kevin Hart, get a gold medal at the Junior Olympics in your first year competing, and I've heard your teacher describe you as the "calm in the midst of chaos." You make me the man I am, and I will never stop being the father you come to know and love.

Thank you to one of the greatest humans I've known, the late great Lucille Hurston. (a.k.a., Granny.)

I could not exclude someone who is a part of everything that I am—someone who gave all she had no matter what, even after her paralyzing stroke. Granny amazed me by her will just to make sure I was okay.

From my perspective I absolutely would not be who I am if I didn't have my Granny. I always wanted to make my Granny proud, and I hope she's looking from up above and giving me the same warm smile that she used to give me when she was here.

To the men I know personally who are the definition of a great father and are a part of changing a long-standing narrative, I salute you and you inspire me.

Continue to set the bar high and be an example to others who may need guidance and don't fully understand how wonderful it is to have children enjoy their presence.

To the others who I've had conversations with, helped me push the needle forward, and had any part in empowering and encouraging me, thank you.

You know who you are, and from the bottom of my heart, thank you. I've always wanted to help the world in some way, and I feel this is my *Think and Grow Rich* or my *48 Laws of Power* for the world of co-parenting. The impact in this life—whether it's a hundred readers or 1 billion—will be felt and change someone's life forever.

About the Author

Terrell Hurston is a debut author born and raised in Los Angeles, CA. With a passion for writing and helping others, Hurston is excited to finally share his work with the world. Not having his mother around growing up and working through a complicated relationship with his father provided him with the capacity to lean on his intrinsic ability to navigate the world despite and through a painful and challenging lens. As a result, he constructed the blueprint for handling tough scenarios, conflict, and disappointment with inner peace and external success.

Terrell is currently studying business at Post University. His debut book, *The Win-Win Solution: A New Approach to Co-Parenting*, is a non-fiction self-help book that delves into the themes of co-parenting, conflict management, and separation/divorce.

When he is not writing, Terrell enjoys being a dad to his nine-year-old daughter, and working out at the gym where he can zone out and clear his mind while improving his health and physique. He is a proud member of Phi Beta Sigma fraternity and a licensed real estate agent. He is grateful for the opportunity to share his work with readers and hopes to continue writing and helping parents achieve peace for many years to come.

www.ingramcontent.com/pod-product-compliance
Lightning Source LLC
Chambersburg PA
CBHW050655160426
43194CB00010B/1953